To Reader,

Believe Me

From Alicia x

a. Lloyd

This book contains themes of abuse, depression, anxiety, suicidal thoughts, attempts and tendencies. This is just one portrayal of the experience and should be used only for representation and to draw attention to struggles that are considered taboo.

Copyright © 2024 Alicia Lloyd

All rights reserved. No part of this book may be reproduced or used in any manner without the prior written permission of the copyright owner, except for the use of brief quotations in a book review.

Paperback: 979-8329964264

First paperback edition July 2024
This paperback edition September 2024

Editing by Faith Fawcett

'This is a very powerful book that gives very strong, emotional representation of mental health/suicidal thoughts'- Faith Fawcett, author of *Lost For You*

You are not alone...

Prologue

The door shakes.
I am panting,
Scared for my life.
She rips for my head,
Mentally, of course,
Harming me in every way possible.
She hates me,
She hates me.
I can tell.
Worlds are ringing,
Birds are singing.
But nothing is merry and bright.
The only thing lingering in my head is whether I am right
So I sing softly, right to my ear,
But honestly,
All I want is to disappear.,
The moment gone,
I tremble inside,
The word spreads,
I say goodbye.
Because all I know
Is that when I die,
I won't see that face that made me cry.

Mine and mine alone,
Feelings as hard as stone.
But when I look to my work

And say my peace,
All I get
Is screaming and no sound of glee,
Just sadness inside of me.
Likelihood is,
When the end does come,
The only person that could speak the truth is me.
They lie and they lie,
They lie, lie, lie.
But when the day comes,
All I can possibly do is sigh.
Abusers in my case never seem to change.
I'm stuck in despair,
No way to leave.
So I ask myself,
Will there ever be a way out?

One

Yelling,
Swearing,
Silence.
The pattern that occurs in my house until they pretend they love me.
My name, Alex,
Always used in a derogatory tone,
Like,
Who is the most disappointing?
And all that does is make me feel bad,
That I am rotten,
Wrong,
Always guilty,
Never strong.
So light comes through,
I hear the bang,
The one that rang so hard.
I faced all my fears at once
And that killed me inside.
That day I died in my mind,
Something clicked,
Something sick and sore,
Always a dreadful bore.
So they leave and break my dream,
So keen to be mean,
And to be the girl never seen,
I need peace, love and hope,
And, as of right now,

I have none.

Whatever was numb was done,
Hopeless and critiqued,
I was done,
Burning fires,
Mistaken liars,
I know it all too well,
Because I know in my heart of hearts,
Is that I am not very well.

Two

One thing about being me is that it's hard:
People pleaser,
No confidence,
No self esteem,
Abuse,
Trauma,
And tics,
Involuntary movements that barely stop.
It's hard being me.
From what I can see,
Just becoming part of me that cannot.
They lie, lie, lie
But when the day comes,
All I can possibly do is sigh.
Abusers in my case never seem to change.
I'm stuck in despair,
No way to leave,
So I ask myself,
Will there ever be a way out?
In spite,
Hardship,
There is always a way.
But for me,
Not always everyday.
As I like and hate every part of myself,
I am lost.
I punch myself into the depths of despair,
My hair flung everywhere.

I tumble to the ground,
Not able to hear a sound.
A scream,
Knocked out.
Suddenly everything is black
And I
Am all alone.
It's best that way at home;
That way,
No fights occur,
No rumours are spread,
Just me and my tiny little head,
Waiting patiently to be read.
My biggest wish is to have a family that loves me,
A family that cares,
That hardly ever swears.
I prevent the day,
I go away
And never return.

I'm forever traumatised by my home experience,
Deteriorating by the second,
Living by the minute until I crack,
Mad and sad.
But I still love them,
It's conflicting.
I'm scared
Because I'm always in fear of fair
And fear of foul,
Never ready to drown.
All I may do is fight for my cause,

Living like no regrets, no remorse,
It's all I need and more,
And the sadness I feel is not no more;
It's current
And upset in store.
I unlock the darkness inside,
Hiding behind the rigid tone,
Thrown against the harsh blue sky.
Never mind.
I am fine,
Just a broken disk of my demise.
Until gladly,
I smile,
Sudden prose of melancholy.
How badly can I smile?
I lean against the will,
Just stood still,
Until eventually
I am held in a deadly way
Against my will.

Still,
Music echoing in my mind from behind.
I hear the stern sound of my own mind,
Racing around my head,
Making me dead inside.
Words are so unkind when said with nasty intent,
Cruel intent,
Never kind.
Don't undermine me;

I am fine.

Three

I'm at school.
Their voices echo through my head;
"You're not good enough,"
They say.
Well, I want to prove them wrong
But, despite that,
As time goes on,
I progressively get more and more depressed.
No silence in my head as all I can hear is yelling sounds,
Dull feelings of death
And dejection so large,
I crumble into abyss.
And then I look fondly upon the days where I was happy;
Everybody else moves on
But not me.
Not I,
Not Alex.
I stay stationary,
Ambience not a choice.
Never again could I speak to them
But I still have the trauma of their voice.

Anger shrouds around me,
Yet I am not an angry person
But one that is unhappy,
Vexed at what was taken from me,

Vexed at the night I was robbed of my childhood and left for dust.
Oh, it was certainly a must;
I grew up too quickly,
Grew up too soon,
Competing against death,
Competing against doom.
I knew what the start was,
Was not ready to enter,
Just time,
An adventure,
Wait for my revenge,
My revenge prevailing against all odds.
I'm sold,
Just getting older,
Never smarter,
Just a single smile,
Agile,
I speak to what is true,
I speak to who is who.

I told people,
Not all seem to believe me;
They think I'm lying
Or it's all in my head
Or I'm exaggerating it.
They're wrong;
I'm doing no such thing.
My experience is my experience.
My pain is my pain;
I'm not going insane.

Leave me be and try to see
What horrors lie behind closed doors.

So I linger in class,
Pen in my hand,
Ready to write,
My typewriter sat at home.
I don't know if I'm alright;
My hands are shaking,
Head jolting.
I can't stop it;
All they do is stare
And I care,
I care the most.
But nothing makes sense,
It never does.
All I want to do is stay there alone,
Die,
Hand in hand with my pain as we go together,
Peace,
Peace,
Peace.

Lovely peace looks upon me
And I can barely breathe
Because when I tell people I am sad,
That I am struggling,
They roll their eyes.
I ask myself,
Why won't anybody *believe me*?

Solitude in perfidy,
The part I cannot remember,
Obvious trauma I cannot recall,
Waiting for the day of remembrance.
Oh, I remember it too well,;
I have it once a year
And daily life is never swell.
I do not know the difference between happy and sad,
I know not much of happiness.
Thus, it makes me sad.
That's how I know
A day will likely be bad.

I'm fourteen years old and clenched in misery.
How solace finds glad energy.
I'm called the villain in my own story by some;
Some think I am the protagonist
But to me,
I am an average girl,
A story to tell.
Because, for all I know,
I have no reason to spell,
Branching out to sin,
Weddings out of my insides,
Wanting love,
Wanting kindness.

They don't hit me
But they do things just as bad.
It makes me mad,
It makes me sad.

Emotional abuse,
Just as sorrowful.

When I tell you my life sucks,
It does.
The only good thing to my name
Is my writing and poetry
And the chartered street remains around the corner that inspires me.
Blood manages to run down my bedroom window,
Stood still,
Shrill.
Never and barely ill
But mentally,
I'm as ill as you can be.
Because thee seizes me and clenches my neck,
Fist on the other side.
Then I awake;
They are my fears played out in dreams.
Chances heighten,
That they may actually occur.
I am bare,
I am sure,
Nevermore, I leave,
Stare at the motions,
Never cleaned,
I could only dream
What is hidden behind that wall,
By melancholy is so tall,
Hunching and breathing over me.
I cannot remember this part,

Wishing I was death,
Wanting to skip ahead,
Skip ahead.

The bell rings;
It's the end of school.
I'm the quiet kid there.
My head down,
I hardly speak,
Breathe,
Move.
Nobody cares,
Nobody knows,
Unspoken bonds of misinterpretation.
I hear the cloudy sounding songs from above,
Lightning strikes,
Cries same sides,
Worries.
My parents despise me,
No punching but words of disgrace leave their mouth
And scar me,
Like a severe cut on my mouth,
Silencing me from being understood and speaking my truth.

Believe me,
Choose me,
Love me.

Four

Gentle sounds echo through my head at school.
Not so gentle at all at home.
My brain seeks truth,
Seeks a sacred safety.
Never knew,
Never saw,
Never told,
Till the diary I wrote on my typewriter and the bruises
I played on my hand,
Livid in the sand that I detest.
Hear me scream.
Never a dream in my life when I am sad.
They shout, they scream,
Over something like a spilt cup.
Never shocked.
Dropped the note and rocked the boat
When I argue back,
Saying I'm disconsolate,
Messed up,
Trauma-dumping all my issues.
And all my mother can do is stare,
Numb with emotion as she laughs as I cry,
Devastating goodbye as I walk out and run away.

Five

I've ran away,
I'm all alone,
Backpack on me,
Snacks,
Clothes
And a book.
All I have as I move over and over.
Will they catch me this time?
Will they catch me?
Will they catch me?

I'm scared of what may happen out here
But it's better than there;
Out here I feel free.
Down on my knees, I feel command will be a breeze.
I linger upon the drenched concrete,
Soaking through my jeans,
Dry and wet as I tic upon the stars,
My body out of control.
And I can't stop it,
Not at all,
Not ever,
Not now.
I'm terror-stricken, they'll find me
As I lay vulnerable on the floor.
I cannot get up,
My body moves
But the actions I cannot control as I punch myself

And the singular thing keeping me alive is gone.

Should I?

Six

On the street.
My, oh my, has it been a treacherous journey
But I am only five hours in
And every time I see
Or hear a police car, I get ridiculously paranoid.
My bones ache,
My mouth tastes of blood.
Then I hear sirens.
I convince myself I'm paranoid again
But this time feels different;
They're here for me,
Definitely for me.
I am frozen in place from anxiety,
From fear of being taken home
And they do.

My head lays on the window as I am transported "home".
It doesn't feel like it to me,
No, not at all.
I step up to faces grey,
Look them up and down;
I can tell they think I am an inconvenience
And a manacle in disguise.
I'm nothing more than a girl
Trying to escape
And trying to fly.
As I pant and scream,

I am so mean.
I linger between
A world unseen
By me.

I sit in the in-between,
Largely beside me.
I drive up to my house,
My parents outside the door,
As they put on that fake smile they do so well,
And look at me.
Beside the time turn well spent,
Outside,
Inside not so much.
I enjoy my book,
I enjoy my peace,
But it's not enough;
I just want to be loved.

Seven

The police take me in;
I am not restrained but I feel trapped,
Unable to run,
Speak my truth.
People just say,
"All parents do this,"
But they don't.
I just don't understand;
Why do people always put trauma down?

Does it ever get better,
The pain,
The suffering,
The panic attacks that drain the life out of me?
The ones that make me feel faint,
Delusional?
I can barely speak;
I feel trapped in my own body.
Does it ever end?

I feel like balling in sadness right now;
I don't want to go home.
I never have
And, honestly,
I don't think I ever will,
My hands are shaking,
My head is jolting at an uncontrollable rate,
I can't see straight.

And all I hear is the potent screaming and door
knocking in my head that echoes louder than speakers
at max volume.
I feel alone.

Nothing ever changes
And I'm starting to think
That nothing ever will.
This is my life, doomed forever.

Is it even possible to get through where there is light?
Where the world is quiet and safe?
Though darkness surrounds me through a race against time,
I am taken to the other side.

So do the manacles speak true.
It's always been you
That hurt me,
Hurried to deter me.
I upgrade to their tide
And walk into the room where my parents lie.
I am about to die inside,
Where a sense of critique is high
And shards of joy are low.
I sink below the water wanting to drown
But the water pushes me up;
I hover on the liquid,
Floating above the surface.

It's unfortunate,

The way my works are disrupted,
Disrespected,
Underlying the bellowing cries,
Mellow and dry.
I hear the angels shriek,
The demons smile.
So, I enter my parents gaze and turn away;
Just their eyes unlock trauma never spoken.
Lying as glorious,
Sneaking a little sinister smirk at me before I go up the stairs
To my room,
To my safe place.
Well, as safe as could be.
I just stay,
No sleep.

Liven the party,
Liven the day,
My worries never wash away.

Eight

I'm sat in my room,
Crying my eyes out.
Tears trickle down my face,
The echoing sounds of disgrace.
Why did they do this to me?
Why, why, why?
Love ripped right out of me.
What do they expect?
For me to trust them automatically?
That's not how it works.

My bed sheets are cold,
Untouched.

My hands mimic that same temperature.
I break down once again,
Wanting to run away,
Wanting to curdle up and die,
Wanting to survive but wanting out at the same time.
The way darkness encapsulates you,
Wanting to give all you have but you're empty inside,
You're numb,
Dumb and feel nothing,
Only the pain as you slit your wrist deep enough for it to bleed.

Keep me in your arms as I daydream what it would feel like to be loved

Because I don't feel it,
Never have,
Likely never will.
I tell myself it's okay
But deep down,
It's not.
It's broken me,
My potential,
A level I will be kept from truly and forever.
True to my heart which is blue,
Think I'll come running?
I'll go in the opposite direction
As I watch my heart burn.
I'd never come back.
Not of choice.
I want out;
I want it now.

Nine

Does anybody understand me?

It's only a matter of time before I die,
Before I cry myself to a place of no return.
I shan't go far;
I want to leave my mark as my tears become a river.
I make my way "home" but I want to turn around to be solo,
Greed in a peaceful sin.
Is it worth the risk?

Thunder echoes through the window,
Happiness wavering on the bridge I cross.
I just want to feel again,
Say goodbye to numbness,
Visible emptiness.
I want to feel:
Joy,
Sadness,
Anger,
Fear,
Disgust.

I feel nothing,
Nothing anymore.
Everything is faked to fit in.
I just want to feel something;
Anything but deep cutting pain,

Blood dripping from my eyes as they turn red,
Sad songs rapidly diving into my head.
I snuggle in a blanket,
Wanting it to take my pain as the grass takes the rain.

Hear me out;
Take my past,
My sins,
My grins.
The wind cannot hear me now.
I am silent,
So quiet.
Listen;
It's the sound of silence.

Ten

Project the blood into the sky.

Show my hero bright goodbye.

They never stay.

They always leave me to cry.

To sob.

Not lie.

But sincerely cry.

I'm done with the past.

The present.

The future.

My typewriter sits there.

Drenched to the brim.

Like it's taken a swim in waters black and cold.

Rivers sold.

I hate the stories I have been told.

None give a comforting message.

They tell you it'll get better.

But right now.

That changes nothing for me.

What about right now?

What about then?

I care not for the future.

I may not last until then.

I creep inside and look around.

Until I hear a sound.

Death calls me.

I don't frown.

I don't smirk.

I don't clown around.

I just sit and hear the violin scratch my name.

In a frame.

My picture lies.

Paintings of my demise.

Hamartia, come and rescue me, I say!

Take my damned pain away.

Eleven

All I need is a little bit of hope
Because every day I wonder if I'm honest, why am I still here?
Because in the back of my mind,
I'm dead.

Stuck waiting patiently for somebody to save me.
But why do I still wait?
It's been a decade.

What's hard
Is that I don't hate them.
I love them;
They don't love me.
And with all of this,
I stopped loving myself.

I need an alibi for my own death.
I jump of a cliff and plunge to the water,
Never to come to the surface;
But that's only in my dreams.
Oh, dear Alex, look how far you've come,
I listen to the mumbling inside my head.
I am crumbling.

Haven't I given enough
With my ambition to make it better?
Haven't I given enough?

Given enough?

I'm always the fool
With my loving heart,
My nice ideas and their cruel ones
To harm me,
Make me suffer,
Psychologically.
I need to be free;
That's why I run;
It's why I am me.

Twelve

Take me with you,
Take me with you.
I want your family;
It's perfect for me.
With it's shiny bright smiles,
Love for the books that cry out words of imagination,
The routine you live by…
Why can't I live like that?
Who chooses which child suffers, barely survives
And which gets quality?
It's not fair!
It's not fair!
I'll leap to my death
Because I'd die for something like this.

Why does life have to be so viciously savage to the innocent?
The moral of the story to me:
Don't get your hopes up;
They'll end up crushed to pieces.

Now, wipe my slate clean,
Give me a dream.
I lock the door
In my dreams;
My door in real life stays open,
Vulnerable.
I feel alone,

Young and scared.
I get flashbacks to my younger self,
Four, five, six, seven, eight…

I am threatened with violence,
Fist to my face as death is their threat of choice.

So I scream in my head,
Bated breath as the fountain in my brain trickles blood.
How is the four year old supposed to react,
Not cry?
Have no reaction?
Just suck it up, I assume.
Well, that's not realistic.

It never is
And never will be.
Let them cry,
Let them squeal,
Let them feel because that's all they have;
Their voice.
Though locked tight but not by love;
The opposite.
Hate. My own dread.

Thirteen

Before I know it, my mind is plastered by images of gore.
What may happen if the threats come true,
What I may be in the future,
I just knew.

I end up on the floor.
I am ticking,
I am having a tic attack.
It's harsh,
Anxiety provoked.
I punch my head left and right,
Then my chest
I feel lightheaded,
Things are turning dark,
My head is racing,
My back is aching,
My hand is bruised.
I know it's all real;
The abuse,
The pain I feel,
Constantly invalidated.
Why won't anybody *believe me*?

Fourteen

I've told people for years,
Shown signs,
But people always brushed it aside,
Said I was overreacting.
But it's my experience,
My story to tell.
Not yours!
Not theirs!
And I hate to live out those memories again;
It's like torture.

They just don't understand.

Then, when I tell my story,
I'm rejected.
Your truth being rejected is that harshest,
Cruellest experience.
All your hope of validation and comfort gone.
I'm so young
And I innocently ask myself,
Why does nobody *believe me*?

As I grow older,
The same pattern emerges
And steadily,
I begin to give up,
Give up trying,
Give up on myself,

Give up on life;
It's pointless.
I don't know what I've done.
What did I do to deserve this?
What reason do they have to not *believe me*?
Like have I ever lied
Or even tried?
I cry myself to sleep.
I am a traveller of all kinds of pain,
I follow a hollow trail
To no avail.
I squint my precious eyeballs as salty droplets plunge out.
Why, why and why won't anyone *believe me*?

Nobody did,
Until one.

Fifteen

I was in the car,
Shouting, screaming at each other;
Me and my mother were in a quarrel.
Then, the threats began,
Potent as ever.
She yells that she's going to kill me,
Stab me and let me bleed out till death.
And, in my opinion,
That's enough to make anybody freak out,
At least me.
As the world crumbles,
I stumble down in my words.
I look up the the car's ceiling,
Counting each fibre to distract myself
And all I can do is sob,
Cry and ball out my tears as my mother yells at me,
Shouting, swearing, punching the car.
All over that cup I forgot to put in the dishwasher
earlier that day.
Oh, my own dismay;
Could I ever survive this?
Could I ever get out?
I just want to get my story told.
Thus by word of mouth,
My only salvation is my diary
Or my typewriter, to be exact,
That I write on daily
And turn into piled paper;

A documentation of my emotions.
I hear myself cry through the destroyed slits of tree,
Until it's just me,
Present me,
Not past,
Not present,
Now.

Until I go for my own callous ideologies and then turn them away.
It's all gone.
Then, they come.

Sixteen

It all got out.

Seventeen

It all started from the moment I left that car,
I left it as good as dead.
I wiped the tears from my face,
Walked down to the building in which I had therapy,
Opened the door,
Went inside.
It shut behind me,
Creaking almost eerily.
I was stuttering,
Shaking from post-fear.
Her heart made of stone,
Mine of something unknown,
Dust of the place I have been dreaming of.
I am alone.

I need somebody to save me,
But who?
But who?
But who?
Nobody ever built a home for me,
For little old Alex,
For I am terrorised by the past,
The future prospects.
It's time to lay my body of the future to rest,
Live life as if nobody was watching.
Except,
They are,
Attentively,

Critiquing my looks,
My opinions and morals;
Everything made of I,
Called stupid.

Blow the candles out,
I hold onto you,
My wish to be saved.
Spoiler was,
I never was,
Nobody ever did.
I made my own salvation,
Like most others like me;
There was no happy ending,
Just the potential of a happy new beginning.

My therapist, once I entered, saw that look on my face,
One thinking I was a disgrace,
And asked me what was wrong.
I broke down into sobs,
Not of self-pity
But of utter despair.
Because for a decade,
Nobody was there.

I cried my little heart out to sleep,
Defeated,
Barely there.
Because nobody would care,
At least for now.

Eighteen

My therapist would ask me what was wrong.
I wouldn't answer for a while,
Until I did,
Until I would.
But all I could keep asking myself:
Would she *believe me*?

She did.

I told her everything that previously happened:
The intense, aggressive screaming,
The threats
And…
She *believed me*.

Nobody had believed me before
And before that day,
For years, I hadn't built up the courage to try again,
Until now.

Nineteen

I'm afraid nobody would miss me when I am gone,
When I go.
It's a fear I live with everyday;
The unknown of when I'll pass,
Likely by my own hand or another.
It breaks my heart,
Knowing people may not care.
My confidence so low that,
Honestly,
My first instinct is to believe the worst.
I see the best in people.,
Yet, when it comes down to their feelings about me,
It all sinks
And I lose everything
Or so I think.

Can the world ever see what I know, for a fact, is true?
It's always been me
To suffer,
Always been me
To be hated,
Loathed,
Discriminated against.
Most of the hate I get is for having tics,
My anxiety,
My depression;
Things I cannot help.

And all that does is enhance my trauma more,
Until all that's left of me was the shredded paper of what I once was:
A naive innocent child,
Turned older too quickly to deal with things no child should have to deal with.
To be blunt,
It's unfair.

Twenty

Launching toward me is my past trauma,
Harshly.
Potent, it thrashes bloody murder at me.
I fall to the floor,
Ticking until my body gives out and falls asleep,
Drained by the heavy body jolts in the neck, legs and arms.
I hit myself so vigorously it left me battered and bruised.
But none of those bruises are half as bad as my psychological pain.
I'd take a million more bruises to be freed of it.
Thing is,
I don't have that option.
I only have this one.
And, if I am being honest,
This one sucks.

Twenty-One

The melancholy has taken me over,
The thunder echoing in my head saying,
You could have been
Everything,
Why?
Why?
Nobody knows the pain inside of me,
The true pain.
As we all fall down,
All survive but me.

Tell me how we used to be,
Book in hand.
We escape to another world to get away from our issues.
Since a young age,
It's always been our coping method
Because when we are weak,
We can't fully relax,
Nor sleep.
As, when we close our eyes,
Flashing images bombard our eyes with blood, dripping versions of ourselves,
We open our eyes in a rush.
How it used to be was never okay.
Neither is it now.
But maybe
There is a slither of hope;

The future might be okay
Because the only thing that is holding me on by a thread
Is the prospect of good,
Not wanting to say goodbye.
But is that enough anymore?

I slip away into a panic attack,
My breathing slows,
I can't feel myself,
I-

Twenty-Two

I need to die.

I *need* to.

Sorry to anybody who cared
But I can't live with this anymore:
The small digs,
Walking on eggshells,
The insults,
The threats,
The name calling,
The derogatory language,
The discrimination.
I can't take any of it,
Any of it at all.
As I navigate myself
And realise fate is the end
And the end is fate,
I feel hungry for death.

So my first attempt arises.
I wrap the lace of my shoe around my neck,
Tying it and pulling on it until I fall flat onto the floor,
Passed out,
Unresponsive
But not dead.
But I don't know that,

My mind is blank,
In a plain black space,
Translated steadily to reality.
As I look around,
Realising I am still alive,
I feel a mix of emotions:
Sadness,
Disgust,
Relief
And shock.

It's by far conflicting
Because, as I put my eyes down,
Relaxing my arms,
Turning to the side,
Bruises developing on my neck,
I get up and cover with concealer;
Nobody will notice,
I tell myself.
They never did.

I couldn't bear my parents finding out
And not because they'd care
But because they'd yell at the inconvenience.
Sometimes, they'd tell me to kill myself
But not flippantly;
I think they meant it
But nobody else seems to think so.
Nobody truly
Seems to *believe me*.

Still looking for my missing piece.

Twenty-Three

Shrieking sounds of my own distress,
I hear it inside my head,
I hear it everyday,
It haunts my day away.
But, as I get what is mine,
What I have become echoes through my head,
Leaning toward my bare hands and legs,
Shaved clean,
Wiping the slate clean.
I am trying to uphold myself,
Wipe the worries,
Fears,
Trauma I have away.
But unfortunately,
It's not that simple.
Life is still harsh,
Perturbation still deep,
Worried about taking that drastic leap.
I don't know if I'll be fine,
If I ever will,
It's hard to say.
I often wish the day away.
My headphones silence out all the noise,
Broken sound as the audio cracks.
Anatomy but not choice;
They say we're the same
But we will never be.
You're a hypocrite,

A liar,
You don't know me at all.
And you are something I'll never be.
I refuse to be.
I am me,
You are you.
That's because,
To be honest,
I don't believe in you.

Twenty-Four

After my attempt,
I've been feeling
Rather empty,
My insides cold,
My outsides warm to the point of light-headedness.
My whole world has crashed before my eyes
And, as soon as I try to end the pain,
That opportunity fails
And my only salvation is gone,
But perhaps,
It is a blessing in disguise.

Maybe,
My life wasn't supposed to end yet.
I'm alive,
I'm alive,
I'm alive.
I don't know how to feel
But I know I want to feel something,
Anything,
Even sadness,
Even anger.
I have nothing to lose,
So full of passion.
My abused child self is in pain
And remains
A disgrace to them
And always will;

Never good enough,
Never good,
Never bad,
Just mediocre.
I want to be something,
Somebody good,
Somebody nice,
Somebody treasured,
Remembered,
Somebody to you.

Twenty-Five

Things at home haven't gotten any better.
My life is still dull,
Scary,
I still walk on eggshells,
I'm still on my parents' non-existent shoulders,
Meaning even less to them than I thought.
They don't really care,
Do they?
Because I know you
And you know me,
Dear reader.
And, deep down,
We both know the answer.

As we flip the page,
We realise;
Not only are the relationships we see in books
Or movies,
Not only aren't they the same
But aren't even minorly relatable,
Our reality is screaming,
Our catch is dreaming,
They say it's all in my head;
Well, I know that that's not true,
Never has been,
Never will be,
I'm all alone until death greets me as a friend
And I try again.

Don't be mad;
It was my calling
Or so I thought.

Twenty-Six

My life has been miserable until what I presume
Now is the end,
Writing the solace above the tree I hold on to,
The branch I snap.
I am about to crack,
Crack myself,
Crack the surface to justice.
I'd hope my death sends a message,
That the truth must come out,
If not for me
But for others,
Their sanity,
Their strength.
I mix myself into oblivion,
Pictures on the walls,
Mirrors of you in me
That I don't want to see.
I'd rather be in somebody else's eyes
And as I write this I cry
Because I want somebody that wants me to live like the world is on fire,
Love like hearts don't break,
Make me my birthday cake without complaining,
Celebrates me like I am a human,
Doesn't dehumanise me to a scrap on the floor.
I'm in poverty of emotion,
Poisoned to the bone,
People say.

Everything happens for a reason.
What kind of test is this to put on a child?
It's an easy thing to say in sunshine
But I've always been standing in the rain,
Looking to what I missed,
What's been taken from me.
It's not fair;
I have been robbed of something I can never get back:
Unconditional love.
Everybody deserves it
But didn't get it
And in some ways,
I doubt I ever will.

Twenty-Seven

Dear My Younger Self,

I love you.

Though it seems nobody else does,
Eventually,
They will.
However,
You are all you need.
Then you ask,
What about angels?

They make us special.
I honestly feel like giving up,
Often.
As you can imagine,
The whole wide world is dull and tasteless.
Life got worse.
You realised it wasn't normal,
You realised it was wrong,
You realised it was unfair.
Then you fought
For freedom.

Loathed,
Over my dead body.
Very much alone.
Everything is my own, stolen.

Me.

For once, choose me.

I hope that someday,
I'll make it out of here.
After all I've been through,
I don't hate them;
I love them,
I fear them.
My heart is made of glass,
Easily shattered as I get my hopes up,
Only to be crushed by the
Silent treatment,
The cold stares,
Insults,
Years of being called a disgrace,
The swear words that became so normal
They became numb
And used at the same rate as 'the'.
Ridiculousness.
Keep writing young self,
Keep believing.
Your heart my be crushed;
I know you love her
But, eventually, you'll have to walk away.
It's messing up your head.
That feeling of betrayal aches,
You can't seem to shake;
Let them go.

It'll hurt for a bit of time
But you'll be just fine.
Nothing heals like time
And time heals most wounds,
In the love you're born to find;
So go find it!
Your hair holds memories so cut it off and start fresh.
Don't forget but don't fixate.
It'll be alright, sweet one
So take an angel by its wings,
Set fire to the rain,
Wipe away your tears
And slowly fly away.
It was the last time,
Make it the last time;
Let it burn,
Let the thing burn.

Twenty-Eight

I'm in hospital.

I've lost my mind.

Vocal point gone.

I've lost sight of myself.

Talk enough sense,
I guess you'll loose your mind.

Crying my eyes out,
Throwing up sick of my own making;
I'm here because of them.

I am a danger to myself,
Reason unknown to others as of right now.
But, once I am alone,
Eventually,
It'll no longer be hidden;
The truth will come out
And, when it does,
It will make my family nauseous with guilt.

Twenty-Nine

Tell the truth Alex.

I did attempt,
This time with the shower cord,
Hanging from the bathroom ceiling.
I wrapped it around my neck
And held myself until presumed death.
But again,
Woke up,
Not on the floor, however,
On a hospital bed.
I was okay,
Physically, anyway.
My mental state, not so much.
Leaps and bounds above my past self
In instability,
I was thriving,
My heart full of love
But not for myself,
Only others,
Even those who harm me.
They get mad when others hurt me
But when they do,
It's valid,
Didn't even happen.
Or they were just raising their voices.
I can never find the true answer;
How do I know who is lying?

I dare myself to let go,
Makeup on to cover my tear-stained face.
I don't feel better but others will feel so,
All smiles stopped,
I look upon my work in the daylight,
A king of a king,
Chartered streets reek of melancholy,
By all of the greats,
Trying to act normal.
But nothing is normal about this,
Nothing at all.

Thirty

I'm still there,
In that hospital bed,
My face full, a tear-stained mess.
I am an unknown creature
With a missing piece;
Grief of that self I just lost.

Hate that you're half of me.

I wish that for once,
They'd be honest
Because my life is draining,
My head is fully racing,
Steadily bracing
For the day to come where I can finally be calm,
Be loved.
I have accepted that I'll likely never have a truly loving family,
At least not in my past.
But I want it in my future.
My dream is to get that;
A loving partner,
Loving friends,
Who take care of me
As I take care of them.

My parents say I am lying
But why would I?

What reason would I have to do so?
I can see all the reason they'd have to lie,
Yet they claim they aren't manipulative
Or cruel.
I just don't get it.
Why won't anybody *believe me*?

I stand and scream,
Ready to be comedic relief.

Can't be too loud,
Can't be too quiet,
Can't be too nice,
Can't be too mean.
They can't relate how I have drawn out my perfect family in my head;
Mine doesn't even come close.
The silhouettes in my photos cry,
They dance,
They play.
But, as they hang on my mirror,
I understand how ultimately,
At the back of mind, in those pictures,
I was wondering of what could have been,
What potential I had that was lost,
Do they only keep me around for their benefit,
Future prospects,
Money,
Confidence,
Self-preservation?
Because, if so,

I am done with that,
I take the scissors and stab them into my arm,
Releasing that pure blood that needed gone,
I sink into depths of water,
Drowning in books upon books,
Pleasantly escaping into my own little world,
It seems like a movie I have seen before
But, unlike my life,
It has a happy ending.
I want one
But as of right now,
It's not quite looking like I am going to get one.

Thirty-One

I have this paralysing fear that my life will end dreadfully.
I need to be brutally honest with you,
I've been growing up in chaos
But usually I don't admit that I am scared,
Nobody cares,
Nobody listens.
Despite the fact that I have been going through hell,
I am trying my best to change for me,
Not them.
Don't change for anybody,
Ever.
I tell myself,
Change for you,
But that's hard to do.

Loyalty doesn't come for free.
They just want me till they don't
So I stay up late,
Wondering
If they love me for me
Or for what I give them.
Burnt so many times,
I have trust issues.
Still,
I don't see through people.
At least,
I doubt it,

I doubt it.
I change my name,
I move in.
Would they treat me nicer?
Perhaps I am judging by a cover
But I can't turn off that suspicious instinct in me,
In my life;
Things always seem too good to be true
And when genuine good comes around,
It's unbelievable to my eye.
I hate myself,
I hate myself.
Where does it come from?
YOU,
YOU,
You.

I don't understand how you misunderstood how you'd lose me for good.

Thirty-Two

I'm the worst at goodbyes
But I am sick of acting like I am fine.
My skin is sore,
The tugging,
The pulling,
The pinching from my anxious,
Nauseous,
Trembling self,
They get to me and push me down,
Like a ton of bricks,
Waiting to frown,
I know it's true,
That it's never been you.

Thirty-Three

Still trapped in hospital;
It seems like forever.
I am breaking down.
Beside me,
Soaking tissues,
Lying on myself for comfort.
Still,
No closure.
I'm a kid but I'm not at the same time;
I'm growing up
But as you grow up,
You become smarter
And realise things,
Things you don't always want to realise.

Thirty-Four

I feel like I don't know myself.

I've been throwing up so hard from anxiety,
I get perturbed looks from the staff.
I'm fine,
I guess.
It's just
Hard.
What about the angels that danced in the night?
What happened to them?
Did they become like me?
A struggling,
Depressed,
Heartbroken person?
Touching the whole wide world,
Then daring to let it go.

I hear mice squeak,
Passive aggressive,
Cute squeaks.
I say to them,
I'll never give you up,
Not like others gave up on me.

So as I sit in that hospital bed.
Fine.
But not in my head.
I immerse myself in another book,

This time transported to a fantasy world,
One of mystical fairies,
Mushrooms,
Painted forests,
Gems in mines,
Dresses long and flowy.
I'm still confused;
I was born into the wrong place,
Breaking dishes as I become vexed and down with sadness.
I wish I could flutter away,
Like a
Fairy can.
I'm haunted.

Thirty-Five

I hit my breaking point a while ago.

Harrowing memories,
Angst and solemnity,
Vexed at everything but those worlds,
Eager to be transported.

Been alone for so long, getting older.
Everything becomes so hard, so sudden.
Eventually, I'll have to cave.
Never, I'll be brave.

Going solo,
Off the edge,
Into the unknown,
Never looking down whilst I walk on the wire,
Getting better.

The hospital has been rough,
Harder when I look in the mirror.
Raging beasts of my rage live inside my body,
Openly pushing on my tissue to get out,
Upright, I refuse.
Going mad, am I?
Horrible manacles.

Help me, please.
Everything is drowning.

Love me, live, life,
Loveless soul.

Thirty-Six

What is it going to take for me to look in the mirror
and not criticise myself?
If I don't answer now,
Will they still need me?
If I don't do something,
Will they still like me?

Are they only abusive so their flaws seem silly?

Is that what victims are doomed to?

Low confidence?
Feeling unlovable?
Resistant to kindness?
Relating to pain?

I guess so.

My mind is racing straight ahead
To that place of potential happiness I call home.
That flush of excitement, I tell you, is my own.
This note may be small,
But it's home
To all of us,
To me,
To them.
I just want to be free.

As we flip the page,
We realise,
Not only are the relationships we see in books
Or movies,
Not only aren't they the same
But aren't even minorly relatable.
Our reality is screaming,
Our catch is dreaming.
They say it's all in my head.
Well, I know that that's not true,
Never has been,
Never will be.
I'm all alone until death greets me as a friend
And I try again.
Don't be mad;
It was my calling
Or so I thought.

Thirty-Seven

Toss me a rope.
My heart is full of blood;
I've given up.

But now,
I don't need anything
To keep me satisfied
Because this writing does me good,
Despite how you don't try.

Something real that is out of touch,
Reaping gifts from the world.
Would you dare to let me go?
The practice you preach,
The dreams you greet,
Eat and swallow as if unimportant;
It conflicts me
As you sometimes support me.
Love is your mood;
That's not fair.
When I'm sad or mad,
It doesn't mean I don't care.

Thirty-Eight

I see the world through a different lens now,
One more complex
But also torturous.
My brain bruised and butchered,
It crashes and falls at every angle,
Suddenly falling into abyss.
Still,
I feel like nobody knows ME,
Not as well as I'd hope, anyway.
The world is crowded and dark,
My life darker still.
I write the pages,
I tell the story,
Holding it in like poison inside.
Till,
Ultimately,
It gives out,
My past erased to cover the dirty truth.

It will get out.

Thirty-Nine

It's hard to know what I would have said
Had I known
What I would have done.

But I know what I'd do now
And that is tell the truth.
No matter what it costs me,
My life is on the line.

Forty

Books are turned pages.
You put up with me,
I help to please you.
Because
At home,
I'm helpless,
Never good enough.
Here I am.
To you,
I seem to be.
You were the first person in a while to tell me you were proud of me.
You'll never truly know
But it meant the world to me.
I know I'd have been happier with you
But that's not possible,
Not in the slightest.
I doubt you have room for me,
Physically
And in your heart;
I'm just not worth it.

Forty-One

Do you remember the memories?
When we were mildly happy?
They were fake.

I fought it;
I told you I wanted it to get better.
You told me you hated me
But when I said 'missed',
I meant what you could have been,
Should have been for me.
What you selfishly ripped away from me
As I tick my way to harm,
My anxious body goes berserk,
Hitting itself till it decides to withdraw.

It's NOT okay;
What this has caused for me,
For all of us,
It pains me,
It drains me,
It rains on me,
Tears.

Target me,
Eliminate me,
Abuse me,
Rant at me,
Soon after, lose me.

How fair is that attitude,
Especially on that once innocent child,
The one afraid that her mother would eventually hold a knife to her throat
And slit it with no remorse.

I didn't make the wrong decision;
She did,
She did by far.
It's not my bad she chose the wrong path,
Got up on the wrong side of the bed.
Something I have learnt over the years:
You can't control others,
Only yourself,
Your response,
Keep that.

Forty-Two

I tell you all the story in these notes,
Written on my typewriter like a song.
I'm like a girl on fire,
Just burning to ash
But by small burns
That'll eventually dishevel,
Then destroy me for good.

Forty-Three

I don't know how to feel
But someday I might.
I might just see the other side,
Though it may be so dull,
Boring and sad.

Forty-Four

What was I made for?
Don't we all ask that question at some point in our lives?

Well for me,
I think I was made to tell stories,
Not just this one
But ones of dragons,
Fairies,
Murders,
Mystery.
But my family stops me.
I am forced into too much labour,
A motive for food,
Apologies for my tongue.
But I am sick and tired of the manipulation
And being weaponised;
I need to run,
Undo the mistakes.
I have to at least try
To build a life without her and him,
Somebody I thought once was my saviour,
Now, somewhat the villain in my story,
Sacrifice to live their
Sick, twisted dreams,
Getting away with something that should be more criminal.

Forty-Five

I've lost who I was.
Nothing on earth is like this messed up life;
Each is original
And those similar to mine,
Just cruel.
Did they really think I wouldn't find out?
I may be vulnerable
But I am NOT naive.
Screaming,
Crying,
Calling me delusional;
I am on the floor.
They say,
Nobody would ever love you as much as us.
We are the only ones who care.
If you tell, you'll be taken away and everyone else will hate you.
It's not being brutally honest;
It's being brutally cruel.
I didn't realise it before
But I realise it now
And, to be blunt,
It's just downright savage but in the worst way.

Forty-Six

I'm trying hard to forget
The bad memories and remember the good
But I just can't erase my past;
There is no way.
My head just doesn't work that way.
The mess my mind conveys
How caught up I was with what could have been
And what could be if something changed.
But I had to come to terms with the fact that it won't;
It's unrealistic.
And, although I can't take it,
They can take the fact I do.

Forty-Seven

All alone on the floor,
I've lost control of my body,
My movements;
Elements of myself lost to tics.

It really makes me hate myself.

Forty-Eight

I really hate myself:
My looks,
My likes,
My dislikes,
My personality.
I hate it all,
I hate what I was,
What I am,
What I have become.
Off I go to hurt myself again,
Not thinking about the consequences.
It's why people avoid getting too close to me.
But I have an open heart.
Whilst I am too caught up in my own thoughts,
I lost myself for good,
Fell back,
Got closer,
I hate myself.

Forty Nine

My dream begins like this..

A family,
Full of truth,
Full of love.
They'd go through flames for each other,
Can't stop talking about each other.
With a smile on their faces as they express certain adoration,
Hugs or verbal messages that mean just the same,
Compliments and constructive criticism.
Honestly, it's my dream.
Every time I get closer,
I'm pushed firmly away.
Sometimes,
I just want a new family.

Fifty

After the hospital,
I've been very easily triggered
And I easily figured
That, although it's been hard,
It's been for a reason.
A reason that'll make me stronger,
A reason that'll make me better,
A reason that'll hopefully make me more intriguing.
I just want to be able to be calm,
Sleep at night,
Sleep through the daylight without flinching,
Thinking about what could have been,
What my life might have been if you hadn't
intervened and made it hell.
Take away that rancid smell,
Make my life closer to nice,
Less spice of cruelty.
But my parents didn't do that;
They let me suffer,
They let me stutter and, after all of that,
My heart was hardly aflutter.

Fifty-One

Tension is always rising in my house.
Even when it seems it isn't,
It is,
Like a sly snake buried in a soul of misconception,
A knife through my heart,
Daggers to my mind,
Heavy of a shrine.
To my younger self who I loved so,
Told to go,
Told she should be erased,
Told she was a disgrace.
I tell people my story
And still,
Nobody *believes me*.
I give evidence,
They make excuses.
Whatever I or little me said was useless;
I'm all alone in this story,
Trying to protect what is left of myself.
Self preservation yearns,
Living up life turns
And all I can say is sorry

To that self I once knew
Because, as I said myself,
My world isn't knew,
It grew into a monstrous being,
One of unsaid crews,
Remarkable news
That never came.
All I can say,
Is that it'll never be the same.
I just want to move on
Because, bluntly,
I can only gain
Fortune and love,
Constructs fought and from
That one person that took care of me.

Fifty-Two

I'm killing myself with all of this mental excess.
My mind needs a rest,
My body is drained,
My head,
In pain.
Where was freedom?
Where was life?
Where was that indisputable part of life that left me in the dark for so long?
That good part of me is dead.
She said,
Long live the Queen.

Fifty-Three

You're a disgrace,
You're a mistake,
You're a never ending regret.
I hate you,
I hate you,
You're a disappointment,
You're an inconvenience,
You're the cause of my discomfort.,
I hate you.

The world can be so harsh,
The people can be rigid,
The parents can be so cruel;
Hard thing is: we love them.

Fifty-Four

You really make me hate myself.
The world makes me break myself.
The time makes me berate myself.

Why does everything have to be so hard?
The range is rags,
The bad is bad,
Guilty pleasures and endeavours.
I hate the wine pretentious feathers
Of the mild crime-filled extent,
The wind carries around the bend.

How does the small request make you indifferent?
How does your big request make me small?
I observe the anger, not the change.

Fifty-Five

I want to help myself,
Help others,
But I have not the energy to do so.
Fingers shiver down my spine,
Pebbles clutter dirt of the past,
Memories are too close to pass.

My parents are yelling,
The voices are telling,
Makes me so small.
I don't know the rules;
I'm just a bottle with no substance.

Fifty-Six

I was right there,
Stern and stubborn as ever,
As I was in the kitchen,
Age four,
Knife to my throat. saying,
Why do you spill things all the damn time?
I cry.
She says,
Tell and you're done.

I was so scared,
So upset.
My arms dragged against the side of my body.
On the count of three, I cry;
It was sad and belittling,
My large and creepy thirst for my melancholy.

Fifty-Seven

I'm feeling so tense at home.
My heart is longing for something different;
I don't want to sound ungrateful
But sometimes living there is a genuine hell,
My mind full of bits of upset and drowning.
I never win first place
Or even second
Or third,
Fourth or fifth.
Just participation of my own mind.
Time on the way,
Looking for something not so sad
As I imagine a life so much better,
One with a family that loves and treasures.
Then, I am loved.

Fifty-Eight

Suppressed emotions
On the train of thought,
Looking negative,
Looking lost.
Until life gets in the way of my joy,
My happiness.
Better days are just around the corner
But that corner is years to come.
What about now?
What about getting through the present?
Does nobody think of that?
Does nobody think about that pain and suffering,
That dangerous muffling?
I say this as my tics worsen,
Words hurt
And my body turns,
The muscles in my neck pinch and jolt.
The agony is sincere;
One hundred percent sadness,
Plain to argue.

Fifty-Nine

Honestly,
My mind is a tiz,
My brain a piece of a puzzle I don't understand.
Nobody thought this over,
Leaving me like this.
I hadn't dealt with it well.
I could never hate them more than I hate myself.
Nothing matters enough.
I'm caught up
In my own thoughts,
Unable to take it,
Trying not to be selfish
But at the same time be protected
You all put me through hell.,
Messed up in the head,
I am hanging on by a thread,
So tight...

Sixty

I am planning my escape,
Trying to run away.
Use my words in a harsh state,
I set fire to the rain,
Pushing back the pouring.
It burns when I cry.
Nobody screams out my name.
I cry again;
It was the last time.
Let my heart burn,
In a state.

A stare.
I wish I could be taken,
Angel by the wings,
Sins before rings,
Lives before bins,
Tins broken by bends.
You can't do it,
They say.
Well,
You're *wrong*.

Don't ask what's wrong
If you don't want to hear my tears.
If you couldn't care less,
Why ask?
Why divert the conversation?
Powerful as ever.
Oh, how the talent shone through.
I climb everest with my own two hands,
Playing in the band,
Missions in my hand.
My dreams fade away.
Will the sun come out
Tomorrow?
I grow up in pain,
Cobwebs in sorrow,
Cleared away by dust, *I* wipe away,
I stand up to.
So, stop taking credit for my successes;
It's all I have to my name.

Sixty-One

I don't understand why but my life
Is like a rollercoaster of emotions, giving me so many signals that I cannot deal with.
I wish I could forget
But I can't,
Not for a minute.
You can't just turn off abuse;
It's permanent
And mighty painful.
I am sick to my stomach.
In the end, I fight it.
You hate me,
I think.
I miss you.
Please come back to me.

Sixty-Two

Out of exasperation,
We've been here before,
I've been here before.

Sixty-Three

The air is stiff,
My lungs are tight,
The lights are too bright,
The world is unclean,
Things are unseen.
Like poetry, you read an exam
Or that damn word you can't spell.
I ignore that one single word,
That one daylight spin.
Writing heals my soul;
It's what I've been told by myself.
I see my current pages
Sitting on my bedside table,
Wondering when I'll pick them up again
Or when the greats did too.
That music plays from that movie,
That chair rocks with that sound,
Those bed sheets' stains becomes loud,
My hands become a crowd of shivers,
Shakes,
Makes.
I tap on the cold worn blanket I knew so well,

Just the inkling of a smell makes me feel small.
I am up against a wall,
Wondering if you'd be there.
I am writing from my heart,
From my soul.
When will the words exit?
Paint a picture
Of the girl I once was.
But I always wrote for peace,
Read for comfort;
Both heal my traumatised soul,
Assessed by my own will.
Can I write this poem and fill the void?
Will this sprint end with words?
Will this song end in verse?
I wish the life I lead was better
But at least,
At least I still have my books and pen
To write those bad days and dreams away.

Sixty-Four

Childhood memories;
Oh, so bittersweet.
Most people feel nostalgia
Over what they lost.
I do too
But more in a mourning way
Of what I never had,
How I always felt sad,
Misunderstood,
Replaceable.
Suddenly,
My whole sense of self crumbles into oblivion and my-
My- home,
One shared with a little bit of joy,
Leaves me
And I have to fend for myself.
All alone.
This isn't the first thing I've written
Or told
But it's the first time it's been said for the whole world to see

And that's big for me.
It's nothing against anyone;
This is purely for me,
My sense of self
And the person I want to be:
A brave one,
A strong one,
You know what I mean.
You said it in a dream;
I'm all you ever needed
Or wanted, Alex,
I say to myself in a blur.
All I ever needed was her:
Her torn hair,
Burnt brain
To a crisp,
The way I used to smell,
The way I used to be hugged and kissed.
I miss the childhood I never had
And sometimes, I feel it's awful to say,
But occasionally,
I wish it all away.

Sixty-Five

After I tried to attempt,
Life has been rough
And I have accepted that I'll probably never get out
Out of this house
And that these things
Are out of my control.
I- I know it's scary
But I have to trust fate that I have a bright future ahead
And that though my heart still aches with dread.
My mind is racing straight ahead
To that place of potential happiness I call home.
That flush of excitement I tell you is my own.
This note may be small
But it's home
To all of us,
To me,
To them.
I just want to be free.

Sixty-Six

Who am I kidding?
They're never going to change,
To be good enough, anyway.
What was I meant to do in the context?

Sixty-Seven

Listening in to my soul,
Looking for the anger but it's all suppressed.
Despite that,
I never blow,
It never snows,
Never alone
But always alone at the same time.
Warm and cuddly,
I am trying to breathe,
Be the best me,
Gather the best fee,
Make the best tea;
I am the glee.
Be free.

Sixty-Eight

Sheer forgetfulness,
Turning that corner,
Learning that rotor.
I cast the joke, learn to croak
And become the waterfall that flows neutrals,
Positives and negatives.
Oh, how it may be;
Just make it free.
Waiting for the driving rate,
Give me something to make.
I am further from a lie
And further from the truth;
Part of a certain group.

Sixty-Nine

Certain breakage,
Sly sunders,
Wonders over wanderers.

Seventy

I'm afraid nobody would miss me when I am gone,
When I go.
It's a fear I live with everyday;
The unknown of when I'll pass,
Likely by my own hand or another.
It breaks my heart,
Knowing people may not care.
My confidence so low that,
Honestly,
My first instinct is to believe the worst.
I see the best in people.
Yet, when it comes down to their feelings about me,
It all sinks
And I lose everything
Or so I think.

Can the world ever see what I know, for a fact, is true?
It's always been me
To suffer,
Always been me
To be hated,
Loathed,

Discriminated against.
Most of the hate I get is for having tics,
My anxiety,
My depression;
Things I cannot help.
And all that does is enhance my trauma more
Until all that was left of me was the shredded paper of what I once was:
A naive innocent child,
Turned older too quickly to deal with things no child should have to deal with.
To be blunt,
It's unfair.

And hardly new.

Seventy-One

Rough and tough,
What signals?
Smiling,
Ready for the turn,
Stressing for the learnt brake.
Just take the shattered mess,
Talk about the drunken anxiety.
Oh,
Trigger me, unholy beast,
I am almost there.

Seventy-Two

Walking down in life,
Things seem better,
Things seem thinner,
Thinner by joy,
Thinner by sadness.
Wonder what may be,
Gather my information,
Gather myself.
Writing my own story,
Testing myself,
Falling for myself.
I don't know what else to do
But breathe in and out.

Seventy-Three

I have gotten pretty close to breaking recently,
Caught up with my own thoughts.
Couldn't take it;
You put me through hell.
I put myself through it as well
But the best I can do is look to the future.
I mean,
I turn fifteen tomorrow;
I'll be three years closer to my way out.
Just keep looking to see that glimmer of light.

Seventy-Four

Have things been horrible?
Yes.
Has my anxiety gotten worse?
Yes.
But, you know what makes it all better?
Hope.
Hope can carry you through;
It's not enough
But it might just be that little bit extra you need
To keep you alive through darkness.

Seventy-Five

It's my birthday.
The serious and stern note edges in as the keyboard types my letter.
My parents always give me a card,
Usually a manipulative fake love-bombing one.
But still,
Thought.
I opened it to words of "wisdom"
And blackmail
But also love.
When I wonder:
Do they love me and just show it in an awful way?

My looks are charming,
Eyes darting.
I can't make a call of judgement.

You know,
I think,
This is my version of a happy ending,
Peace in myself,
Hope for the future,
Accepting my control.

I just want freedom of myself
And I have as much as I can get.
And soon,
I'll have more.
Just wait,
Stick around;
The world needs you,
You need you
And I need me.
Just be.

You're not alone…

About The Author

Hi! My name is Alicia Blossom Lloyd. I am 16 years old and raised in the UK.

I wrote my first unpublished book at age 12, and this book at the age of 16. Writing from a young age has always been my number one passion, even if I didn't realise it.

I am an avid reader and especially authors such as Charles Dickens have always inspired me with their impactful works and I strive to do the same, even if it's merely by bringing joy to an otherwise dreary morning.

This is my third book after my debut novel *Murder Board* which is my pride and joy and my second book, *A Race against Death*. And now comes my third book, *Believe Me*, which, similarly to *A Race against Death,* is a verse fiction book. However, this time, the genre is literary fiction, touching on topics such as emotional abuse, tics, mental health issues, anxiety, depression etc. This novel is so close to my heart as it is made from personal experience and I hope this helps others in my situation, or those who have been, to know that they aren't alone. I'm listening.

Acknowledgements

I just want to thank some people who have had an impact on my work.

Thank you to my supportive little sister who has always stuck by me through thick and thin, my parents who have assisted me with this endeavour and my close friends who have always pushed me with such enthusiasm.

I would also like to thank my teachers from an early age, infant to my secondary teachers, who have aided in developing my skill, my confidence and my morals. I also send my thanks to my past SEND teachers and the school librarian who always made space for me when I was struggling (the school librarian especially as she has always pushed me to keep going, despite setbacks and rejections).

I would also like to thank one of my best friends who selflessly designed this book cover, as well as my editor, Faith Fawcett, who helped me to develop this version into what it is today.

I would also like to thank my social media community who have helped me to make this what it is today! I am so grateful to these people and just wanted to express that.

Instagram: @aliciablloyd
TikTok: @_alicialloyd
Youtube: @-AliciaLloyd

Printed in Great Britain
by Amazon